# How I Built a Million Dollar

# Online Store From $600

*Your step-by-step guide*

*to building financial freedom*

*through E-commerce Entrepreneurship*

## By ELLEN LIN

Edited By DEBORAH HARTER WILLIAMS

# Table of Contents

# INTRODUCTION

# What is an Ellen Lin?

I was born in New Taipei City, Taiwan in 1982. Taiwan is a small island on the southeastern side of China with a population of 23 million people. We speak Mandarin and have a very complicated history with China, but that's a different book.

Most people who have met me assume that I was raised in an upper-middle class household, but I was actually born into a poor family. Papa Lin was a salesman during the day and worked in a restaurant at nights making about $900/month in U.S. dollars. Mama Lin was an accountant in a big corporation in Taiwan – she made $166/mo.

I was an accident, Mama Lin said... just 3 months after their marriage, Mama Lin was pregnant with me. She said she didn't even have time to enjoy her life yet.

Mama Lin carried me on her back and commuted to work via bus. There was a baby care center behind her workplace, so I had a place to stay while she was working. Back then the working days in Taiwan were Monday through Saturday. During summer, there was no air conditioning on the bus, which was always crowded as it was the only affordable public transportation back then.

What I remember best was hanging out with my grandpa all the time (my grandmother worked too). Grandpa was my first mentor in my childhood, and the most important person in my life at the time. Grandpa wanted me to become a "successful person" (by traditional definition- success means study well and find a great paying employer) and to be the first one to receive a master degree in my family. Neither of my parents have college degrees.

So grandpa trained me to write and do math before the age I was supposed to learn that at school. He believed that I would become an elite in school by pre-learning everything. During lunchtime, we watched the TV news together. At the end, they always played the stock market report. I remember my grandpa really cared about that part. He told me to pay attention to 3 stocks. If the stock showed green, he was happy. If it showed red, he wasn't happy.

## Video Games, Japan and Me

I had a passion for video games. Back in the 80's, NES was the major console platform in Taiwan. My uncle bought it for me, as he also loved video games. He promised me a new video game if I could get in the top 3 places in my class on the final exam of the semester- and I did. I was highly motivated by a reward system like this.

Since Taiwan was once colonized by Japan, we had lots of imported Japanese products, especially video games. I thought that if I studied Japanese I would really understand the games I was playing. But Grandpa Lin hated Japanese products. He remembered World War II when the Japanese military invaded and bombed his hometown in China - killing everyone they saw. He escaped and came to Taiwan. Most of the population in Taiwan today, had grandparents who escaped from China to Taiwan. There are some native Taiwanese, (equivalent to American Indians) but they're the minority now.

## My father's dream of the United States

Fast forward for a few years. My mother's oldest sister applied for a USA resident card for my mother, and Papa Lin thought it was a great opportunity, but he needed to get my grandparents' approval. When he talked to them, they got extremely mad. So Papa Lin gave up the idea of moving to the United States.

After a few more years, Grandpa started visiting the hospital quite often. He was diagnosed with lung cancer. But he kept telling me he would be okay. On Feb 22nd, 1992, I remember it was Sunday, the phone rang. My auntie picked up the phone and started crying. Grandpa had passed away.

After Grandpa died I slept with my Grandma every single night, because she was afraid that my Grandpa's ghost would come back. I was not sure why she was scared. I had no problem with that idea since I missed Grandpa so much. About a year later my Grandma passed away because of stomach cancer.

We didn't go to United States right after that since my dad had to apply for the work visa. The next year in 1994, Papa Lin went on a visit to Los Angeles by himself to check out the environment. He instantly fell in love with the city, so he decided to quit his job and move there as soon as he could. During this trip he studied franchised retail stores and potential companies he might want to do business with.

Meanwhile in Taiwan my performance at school continued to be good because I had the knack for memorizing - I still thank my Grandpa's training. I attended a middle school near my house, which was known as a place for students who didn't study much. It was easy for me to become one of the top 5 students in the class. Everything was memorization, nothing required real understanding. In the Taiwanese education system, if you have a great memory, you can do extremely well.

There was a lot of physical punishment at both school and home back then. Teachers would beat the student's palms with a wooden stick. Parents would beat you up with any props they could pick up near them. The education system was based on the military style- if you do well, you get nothing because you're supposed to do well, if you don't do well, you get punishments.

I thought this education system was horrible/, until I heard an interview with Dan Pena. Dan is often referred to as the "50 billion dollar man" and now lives in a castle in Scotland. He uses a military style of training entrepreneurs - emphasizing discipline.

Suddenly I realized that a lot of the discipline I have today came from the military style education I had back in Taiwan. Funny how things that seem to be bad can turn out to be a blessing.

## Fresh Off the Boat

In 1996, Papa Lin finally got his working visa, so he quit his job and was ready to move to the states. At that point, I didn't want to come. I was at the age when I wanted to hang out with my classmates and best friends in Taiwan. But I had no choice, so I went with them and cried.

Papa Lin, Mama Lin, my sister and myself - we packed everything in 8 suitcases and moved to Los Angeles. The only thing I packed was my Super Nintendo and all the cassettes I had- video games were my life. Papa Lin had to start everything all over again. He started a new business in an unknown country. It was difficult for him at the beginning but he had been doing research for 2 years before we arrived and had clear strategies for what he was going to do. I'm proud to say he's an amazing salesman and entrepreneur.

But, it was really difficult for me at school because I didn't speak or understand English well. I couldn't understand what my assignments and projects were. The only class I had fun with was math, because I had learned it all when I was in Taiwan. I didn't need to listen to the teacher to understand.

After 3 months of middle school, I went to high school. Finally I made some friends, thanks to the English as Second Language classes. They put all the FOBs (fresh- off-the-boat/newly arrived immigrants) in the same classes- English, History, and etc. The only classes that weren't arranged for an English standard were PE, math, and the elective classes.

Whoa - PE classes! Nobody in that class spoke my language. I felt so alienated. I didn't understand why Americans would change into PE clothes in public. This didn't exist in our culture. And there was a lot of teamwork in the class, but nobody would pick me because I knew nobody. I couldn't understand what the teachers and classmates were talking about, but I knew some of the classmates were laughing at me. I tried very hard to perform well in the sports I knew how to play, which seemed to make them dislike me more. They would say something like "OMG, don't be so serious!" (I could understand this part).

There was one elective class I LOVED so much - Technology Lab. I got to do web designing for the class! I taught myself by reading an HTML codebook that my uncle gave me.

Later I was so happy I mastered HTML code because it's so useful today when I build company websites.

At that time, my cousins lived with us. My cousin Jason was also a huge fan of video games; he played A LOT of video games. I would sit and watch him. He was the one that influenced me to want to work on video games later on. One day as he played Final Fantasy VII on PS1, I was taken with the amazing character animation. I thought, "I wanted to create something that looks like that one day."

## The SAT challenge

All the Asian parents want their kids to go to the UCs (University of California), including my parents. In order to apply, you are required to take SAT I and SAT II. Like most of the Asian parents, my parents sent me to an after school program to study SAT. They assigned practice questions for every single day, and we would take an SAT I practice test every Saturday. The first time I took the practice exam, I got around 840+ (the full score was 1600 back then, 800 for math, and 800 for English). So yes, I got 790 on the math, and maybe around 40 for the English.

The SAT advisor told me I would not be able to get into any UCs with the score.

I needed some intense training on English, and I had absolutely no idea what the teacher was talking about. So I memorized the question bank as much as I could — and after a few years of hard work, I got into University of California, San Diego.

My parents were so HAPPY! I was the first one in the family to go to college!

They were so proud! And I believed my grandpa would be very proud for me too.

I worked hard for it! At that point, I understood that in order to get something I wanted, I needed to work hard to earn it.

## College - Life became tougher

I started UCSD with an Electrical Engineering major. I was probably insane.

The schoolwork became much more difficult. I couldn't handle the math at that level, and there were so many hardcore geniuses at that school. There was also a lot of reading for the assignments. We were required to read 100 pages from the textbook per week. I failed no matter how hard I tried. For the first time in school I felt stupid.

So I gave up working hard - instead I fell in love with Photoshop and editing photos for my friends. Back then, you could find a lot of software programs online in crack versions- so I could download and use them for free. I taught myself Photoshop. Later I found out this was one of the best skills when doing e-commerce because of editing product photos and designing website graphics. And I also fell in love with playing online games on the school's fast DSL Internet service - which made my school grades even worse!

At UCSD, there was an English exam that we had to pass which required writing a short essay. You had 3 chances to pass this exam. If you failed, you would get kicked out of UCSD. If you failed 5 times, you would be barred from all the UCs. What frightened me the most was that there were many Asians who were born in the United States, and they couldn't pass the exam.

How could I pass the exam if fluent English speakers couldn't pass that? I heard a lot about people who got kicked out because they couldn't pass the exam. I knew it would be a shame for my parents if I got kicked out. I finally decided that I would just try my best to pass. If it didn't work out, it was meant to be.

By now I hated school. Everything was so difficult. There was not even one subject I was good at. When I started taking my first major requirement - Electrical Engineering 1 - I knew this wasn't for me. I couldn't understand a single thing. I dropped the class and felt hopeless about what I should do next.

Towards the end of the freshman year, my roommate Michelle brought great news for me. "Hey did you know our school has a NEW major that just launched this year? My classmate was just telling me about this. It's called ICAM."

"I can't?" I responded.

"No, it stands for Interdisciplinary Computing & the Arts," she said, "It's about graphic design and stuff." The next day I changed my major.

Still I had horrible grades for my freshman year in college, and I still wasn't sure what I was doing. Things changed at the beginning of my sophomore year. I was in our dormitory playing video game (yes as always), when my roommate Dana came back from class and shouted "Ellen, do you want to go to Japan?"

This question ignited the fire in my heart. YES I WANT TO!

I'VE NEVER BEEN TO JAPAN, BUT I'VE ALWAYS WANT TO GO TO JAPAN!

She then told me about the exchange student program that our school offered. She said,

"Let's do this together, we're going to study abroad in Japan for ONE YEAR in our senior year!"

But then she told me all the requirements for getting into this program: GPA 3.0 (I believe I had 2.0 at that time); Take 2 years of Japanese at school (I hadn't taken any at the time); Pass the toughest English test (I was still in ESL - English As Second Language); and finish all English requirements (2 writing classes, but in order to take these, I need to pass the English test first.

It sounded impossible at the time. But I had 2 years to qualify and I was so determined that this was going to happen. I quit playing video games; I started to take maximum classes - and summer classes. I was going to try my very best to meet the goals.

It was so difficult. I failed the English test on the first two attempts, but I passed it on the third. Hooray! My writing class professor made me re-take the class because she didn't think I was capable yet. Luckily I re-took the class and passed it during the summer session just right before I left to Japan. But my GPA was only 2.94. I didn't meet the requirement.

Still I walked into the International Student Center to peek at my final result and see if I got in or not. I still remember how nervous I was. I walked very slowly towards the orange building. And THERE YOU GO, I GOT ACCEPTED by the school I had applied for - Sophia University in Tokyo. To make it even sweeter, my roommate Dana also got accepted it.

It wasn't because of luck. I EARNED THIS by doing all the hard work and achieving things I never thought were possible for me. I had always thought I would get kicked out of UCSD because I couldn't pass the English test. But I DID IT! And now I'M GOING TO JAPAN FOR THE FIRST TIME, FOR ONE YEAR. At this point, I fully believed that I could accomplish anything by working really hard. I think this experience in school built up my entrepreneurial mindset even though I didn't really think about my future career at the time, all I focused was - GOING TO JAPAN!

# Japan

Studying in Japan was my reward. I arrived Narita Airport on July 1st 2003. Tokyo was really fun, there were always cool places to go and visit. But after 2 months, I got homesick. It was my first time leaving my family for so long (I had driven back home from San Diego every weekend when I was in college). I missed my mom, I missed my home, I missed my desk, and I missed my friends.... I still remember that feeling.

It was extremely hot in July. There was no air conditioner in our dormitory. I could hear the sound of the cicadas. There was a green collect phone on the hallway of our dormitory, so I inserted the coins in the phone and called home. It was the first time I told my mom how much I missed her. Yes I was very homesick.

Even though I had studied Japanese for a couple years, I still couldn't understand fully. The movie *Lost in Translation* reflects exactly what I felt. It was a very happening city, there was always so much going on, I never got bored, but I was lonely.

In spite of that I had a really fantastic time in Japan. It was truly relaxing and truly stress free except for the language barrier. I would say it was the best year I ever had before I entered the entrepreneurial world. For those of you who are reading this book, if you are a college student or if you have kids in college, I give my highest recommendation for you or your kids to join the study abroad program. It was the best experience ever and prepared me in ways I could not have imagined.

The lesson here is one of success and failure, of being afraid and working hard, of succeeding and being lonely – and most of all discovering that all of my experiences would pay off later.

**Return to School –** Time to think about what to be when I grow up.

I knew web design, so I thought about becoming a web designer. But I also observed that there were tons of people doing that. I wanted to go niche so I could be worth a damn. (I started having that niche idea way back when I was in college). I decided I wanted to become a game developer, so that one day I could get into Square Unix and become a part of the team that makes Final Fantasy. I still haven't completely forgotten about this dream, I will likely make it happen in a different form in the future.

I spent a few months, learned some basics for 3D art creation and was able to find a 3D artist internship at UCSD. I made 3D art for a character in a student film. And I decided that I was going to go to grad school no matter what, because that was what my grandfather wanted for me when he was alive. I needed to make him proud!

Based on my interest in game development, I applied for grad school at Academy of Art University. I applied for the online one, so I could work and finish my master's degree at the same time. A few weeks before graduation, I received a call from my friend Evan. He was working with EA Games as a Game Tester, and he knew that I had passion for working in game development. He said there was an opening for another Game Tester, was I interested?

Game Tester was a temporary job, meaning I could get laid off after 7-8 months. But he said that I might be able to use this opportunity as a stepping stone to becoming a 3D Artist in a game company. I went in for an interview - my first official job interview in a big corporation. I was really nervous. On the interview day, I drove 2 hours to EA Los Angeles. The interview included two parts; the first part was a written test. If I didn't pass the written test, I would not get into the face-to-face interview. Luckily I passed.

Then I was taken to a small room with two interviewers. They asked me at least 10 questions, and I didn't know how to answer some of them. I was very nervous and I thought I performed poorly. How could I not prepare for an interview for a job that I cared so much about? I drove home and felt depressed.

After a nap and I texted my friend Evan telling him I did a poor job in the interview. He told me he would check on the final result. I was so surprised when he told me I got the job. The next day I got the official call asking me to start working on June 13, 2005, just a few days after my graduation.

Being a game tester was every gamer's dream- able to play video games all day long and get paid. But, it wasn't fun. We had extremely long working hours. 70 hours per week, staring at the computer, playing on the same level, repeating the same stuff, logging bugs, verifying the fixes. Over and over again.

Every 3-5 months we had a new project, repeating the same stuff. What excited me was that my name was on the credit list of the game. The job was easy for me because I was fast, and I was one of the top testers on the whole floor of 200 people. I was able to find 20 bugs per day while average people found only 3 bugs. After 7 months at this, about the time I expected to get laid off, EA decided to promote 5 of the 10 top de-buggers to become permanent employees. I was one of them – A Senior Tester.

## 3D Artist

After one and a half years, I was totally burned out by the job. I knew I needed to move on if I was to become a 3D artist. There was an internal hire for a 3D artist position at EA at the time. I applied for it but I didn't get it. My 3D art attempt was an epic failure.

I knew I needed to learn more skills. I found the Gnomon School of Visual Effects in Hollywood and signed up for classes. Meanwhile I was working 70 hours per week, and getting my online master's degree, but I managed to drive to Hollywood to take a 3 hour Game Environment Creation class every Sunday. I had no energy left, but I knew I wanted to become a 3D artist.

After completing the class, it took me 5 months to finish my demo reel. Every night after I got off work at 9 pm I went home and worked on my 3D demo reel until 1 am. I dreamed about polygons and didn't sleep well. But I knew I had to finish, because I wanted to become a 3D Artist so badly.

There were fewer than 50 game developers in Los Angeles, and many didn't post on any job sites. I spent hours every day to find those game developers online. I made an excel sheet to track down each company I found, and wrote down if they were hiring 3D artists. My performance at EA dropped, because I didn't want to be there anymore and my supervisors could feel it.

After a month of job-hunting, I submitted 10 resumes and I finally got one reply from this game studio in North Hollywood. I was so excited. Even better, one of the art directors who interviewed me was a Japanese, she said she was interested in my resume because I went to the same university as the former Japan prime minister. She actually conducted part of the interview in Japanese. I got the job! I landed my dream job. Lucky? No I worked so hard to earn this. It took me 2 years to reach this goal, and who knew my experience of studying abroad in Japan would help me. I knew I deserved the job.

## Jobless

After 2 years, I got bored with the 3D artist job. I came to the realization that I wasn't really a talented artist. I didn't have the creativity to make a 3D landscape that I had never seen before. I had to rely on my art director to draw me the concept art before I could create anything. And it happened to be 2009, the Great Depression. So I got laid off.

And that's where it all really BEGAN...

Before you listen to the advice I want to give you in this book, I wanted you to understand how I grew up, how I was motivated, and how I became disciplined. You will be able to see where my success came from and what part my personality, background and education played. Now you can look back at your own experiences and see what tools you already have to make you and entrepreneur.

# CHAPTER 1

# An Unlikely Entrepreneur

When the economy crashed so badly in 2009, and I got laid off, my dream of becoming an Art Director crashed too. I will never forget that day. It was my 27th birthday. That day after lunch, our project manager came by, told everyone that it was our last day because they didn't have a next project, and not enough funding to keep us on. We got 2 weeks severance pay. I'd been working there for 2 years. Though I heard lots of layoff stories from my friends, I never thought this would actually happen to me. One of my co-workers smashed his Nintendo Wii controller on the ground and just took off. I stayed at work until the end of the day, finishing everything I should have. After work, I called my family, and told them the news.

Everything changed so quickly after that. I'd lost my dream job and I'd lost my motivation. Every morning, I didn't want to wake up, I couldn't accept the fact that I wasn't going to find another job. I kept checking my emails for possible upcoming interviews. I felt empty inside, I felt like a loser. I didn't know what else I could do besides working in the gaming industry. It's horrible when there's no income, even though I got some money from the government, you know it's not enough.

It's really normal to get laid off in gaming industry. So I thought maybe if I did find another 3D artist job, I would probably get laid off again after that project. I submitted tons of resumes. Only a few responded, including Blizzard, the company that made World of Warcraft. But I didn't pass their 3D art test. Finally after 6 months of being jobless, I gave up the gaming industry.

Meanwhile my father's business was in really bad shape, so he asked for my help. On the side, I found a 3D instructor job in a private art school. They paid me $15 per hour. I thought "Seriously? I spent so much on tuition to build my career. I've had years of professional experience in the industry, and I'm worth only $15 per hour???" It's what it's like when you work for someone else. I don't get to decide my own value. Other people get to decide it.

Even though my dad had me helping him, his business was not getting any better, in fact it was getting worse. We were finding out that traditional business operations didn't work anymore in this century because of the Internet.

## Light bulb

So, we thought, the only way out is to use the Internet to make money. And many of my friends were doing e-commerce back then. In 2011, my father and myself invested $600 to buy some small products in Taiwan. We put everything in our luggage and brought it back to the US.

Remember I had no business background at all. I was an artist. Even though my dad had owned a business, his knowledge was only suitable for traditional business. We started an online business without a clue. For our first month, we did $1,000. I was so happy, because it worked! And I started to think "oh maybe making money is not that hard."

We first started with eBay, and then launched on Amazon one year later. Although the business was established by the two of us, it was mainly me who did everything. He was just there nagging.

## Yay, and Oh No!

Our revenue for the first year was $43,000. I was sitting in my garage, staring at the computer. I finished packing up the daily online orders from eBay and Amazon and was trying to figure out how much we might sell this month. I put everything in the trunk, and drove to the post office thinking everything was easy.

And then I suddenly realized one thing - "$43,000! It's less than my salary when I was a 3D artist. And this was the gross revenue - before the product cost and the marketplace commission. Seriously? How could I make a living with this amount of money? It didn't feel right. I had one of those moments of supreme doubt. What should I do? Should I go back to the video game industry? Should I give up this crazy idea of having an online business?

Perhaps you have experienced this doubt as well? I believe it comes to a lot of people when they first start a business. But, because of this doubt, my life changed. I started studying and doing research, kept testing different ways. And finally, I built a formula that works all the time. I call it "The Million Dollar Golden Formula." I'll talk more about that later, so keep reading...

## Fast Forward

In 2012 and 2013, I spent tons of time researching, and I tried to sell popular products. I was so excited because I thought - everybody's gonna buy. But it didn't go the way I expected. I wasted my money.

And I tried advertising, but nobody cared, I wasted more money. I tried different e-commerce platforms. I wasted more time and money. I tried everything I could. How many of you have tried all these but didn't get any results? I believe a lot of you have.

But the good thing is, after all that, I finally found a way that works. Finally in the 4th year of the business, our revenue hit one million dollar, and we did $1.71 million in 2016. Below is our revenue in the e-commerce portion

2011: $43,000

2012: $218,000

2013: $496,000

2014: $1,070,000

2015: $1,420.000

2016: $1,710,000

Our business grew fivefold the 2nd year, and it doubled again in both the 3rd and the 4th year. Based on my success and experiments, I built a formula that can help anyone's online business grow FAST! People who learned this formula don't have to spend years and tons of money on their own experiments, and they can also scale up their business FAST

## Garage Start-up

The picture before is the garage of my parent's house. Everything started from here in 2011 – a one-car garage approximately 260 square feet. In this picture there are about 100 products. Anyway, what I want to say is that most of the big companies started from small garages. Apple, Amazon, Disney, and Google all started from small garages like this. And those famous entrepreneurs were just like us. They were ordinary humans with big vision, and they encountered endless obstacles to get as far as they did.

## The Big Change -

While my life started to change in 2011, it was 2014 when we hit over million dollars in revenue – the change accelerated. Our sales numbers are still growing each year and I am growing as a businessperson.

In 2015, I founded Ellenpro and started teaching people to be profitable online sellers.

In 2016, Kevin Harrington's "As Seen On TV" team asked my e-commerce business to do a video campaign with them. (Kevin is a former shark from the show Shark Tank, and now a very famous entrepreneur.)

As of 2017, our online business has a 9,200 square feet warehouse near Los Angeles.

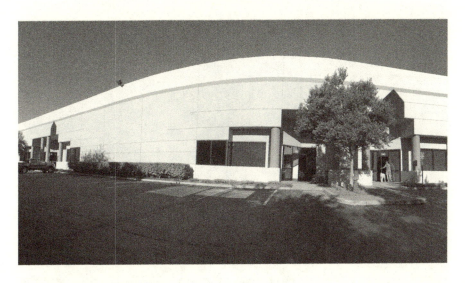

Ellenpro started to take off. I was featured on Grant Cardone TV, The Huffpost, ABC, NBC, CBS, and Fox.

Since then my life has grown and changed dramatically as well. I used to think about where to go after work, what videos to buy. Now I think about how to scale up the business, how to meet more entrepreneurs, what conferences to go to, what books to buy. Entrepreneurship can really change someone inside out. As you can see in the below pictures, I evolved into a magazine model from a monkey.

Besides the financial freedom of entrepreneurship, what I like the most is the time freedom. I can travel whenever I want. I don't remember how many countries I've been to, but there were at least 7 in 2016. I went snowboarding in France, learned cooking in Vietnam, I rode a jet ski in the Bahamas, and hiked on a glacier in Iceland. I also rode a horse to visit ancient temples in China.

## Close your eyes

Ok. Now we have a little exercise, I hope everybody can do this with me.

Please close your eyes, and imagine…

What If?

- You understood all the secrets you needed to build your own million dollar online store, and you actually do it after a few years.

- Your revenue is one million dollar.

What does your life look like?

- You can finally take your family on the vacation that you promised a long time ago.

- You no longer need to worry about the payments and the loans.

- You no longer need to care about what your boss think.

- Your friends think you're awesome.

- You used to fight with your spouse about the money, now you are planning your spontaneous Europe trip together.

- You used to take hours commuting to work each day, now you can work at anywhere you want.

Now you can open your eyes.

Open your eyes to your own possibilities.

This can happen and you can do it.

# CHAPTER 2

# Money and You
# Moving from Employee to Entrepreneur

First of all, if you want to make even more money, you need to understand

"The Game of Money."

Like most games it has different levels.

## Level 1 -Employee

Most people spend their whole working lives as employees, as you can see in this triangle. They work for others. They have 9-5 jobs or get an hourly wage.

At this level of the game, you don't have to be responsible for the company's failure or success. You don't need to worry about if the company's making money or not. And you don't need to worry about work after work.

### But...

*Your time is controlled by your job.*

*Your income is controlled by your boss.*

## Level 2 - Self-Employed

The next level is self-employed, the one-man company.

You are your own boss, you can work whenever you want.

### But...

*How much you make depends on how much you work.*

## Level 3 - Small Business

When you realize that you don't have enough time, you will start hiring employees, and then you become a small business owner. As a small business owner, you have a team of employees.

These employees will take parts of your work, so you can handle more sales, more customers.

**But…**

*Most small business owners get stuck at this level,*

*and they don't know how to move to the next level.*

The reason often is because they think they're the best at what they do, and they don't have people around them who are better than they are. They think nobody else can do the work better than they can. They don't really trust people to do it their way and don't rely on others.

*So it ends up, they do most of the work themselves.*

And what they don't realize is that they are spending most of their time to "maintain" their company instead of focusing on growth.

What if you want to go to the next level? What does it take?

## Level 4 - The Big Company

The secret is to establish a system.

Then teach the system to your employees.

You want to train them in a way that they can do problem solving for you.

Let them "maintain" your company, so you will have time to focus on growing it.

## The Highest Game Level

The very highest level players of the game are investors: Picture someone like Peter Thiel, the venture capitalist, who invested in Facebook at its early stage. After you have the experience of running small and big businesses, and you have a lot of money, you can invest in startup companies and make even more money without getting involved in day-to-day -company operations.

## Mindset

Without the proper mindset, your business will not last long.

That's why most of the self-help books out there are all about mindsets.

No matter what you do, you will find the ways to achieve it if you have the proper mindset. And it will constantly drive you forward.

Most of the successful entrepreneurs in the world, like Warren Buffett, Elon Musk, and

Mark Zuckerberg, study about the fundamental mindsets on a regular basis.

When I first started studying about success formulas, I had no clue where I should go.

I'll tell you more about my success formula in Chapter 7.

## Business Schools

I thought school would teach me the formula for success. So I applied for some online MBA courses from Ivy League universities.

Because I had no business education background, I was naïve enough to believe that MBA classes would teach me about how to be a successful entrepreneur and how to scale my business.

But guess what? While I did get some knowledge, all of the courses really just taught me about how to become a successful employee in a big corporation. Everything was academic and theoretical. So I changed a direction…

## Entrepreneurial School

One day, I saw a Facebook ad about Tai Lopez, investor, entrepreneur and trainer. I signed up for his course immediately and the first thing I learned was the importance of reading. To be honest, I never liked reading before, not even novels. Reading makes me sleepy, really sleepy.

But Tai got me started reading all the entrepreneurial books. That's when the realization came to me - reading makes me sleepy when I don't feel like I'm learning anything. I was bored.

When I really want to learn something, I feel like my reading time is not enough.

I wished I could master speed-reading so I could learn much quicker and learn the golden nuggets from each book.

In the past two years, I have studied many successful entrepreneurs, including the ones from the past centuries. I took online courses, read hundreds of Internet articles, cold-emailed some serial-entrepreneurs, and spent tons of money on conferences. I finally found a pattern from them. I found a formula for a success path. And this formula works on anything, no matter if it's business or a personal goal.

And I found the true purpose of reading. What you learn from books plants seeds in your subconscious. When you need to apply them in your life, these seeds will become flowers in your conscious mind, leading you to make the right decisions.

## Where are you now? Are you one of the following people?

*Sick and Tired?*

Are you sick and tired of being an employee?

You want to become your own boss and control your life and time, but not sure what to do?

*Want to make tons of money but unsure how to go about it?*

Does everything seem so complicated?

*Small Potatoes*

Have you been selling online for a while and made some money, but are finding it hard to boost up the revenue? You might be asking yourself: "Why is it so difficult?

Or it's just that the economy is bad?"

Don't worry. I used to be just like that! It took me years to find the answers.

Many of you want to make tons of money online.

Many of you know the Internet is an amazing thing.

But not many people know what exactly to do.

So just keep reading, I'll tell you everything.

# CHAPTER 3

# What's E-Commerce?

# Where does the money come from?

# What do you need to do to get it?

Let's start with some numbers. This will help you get a feel for the size and scope of what you are getting into.

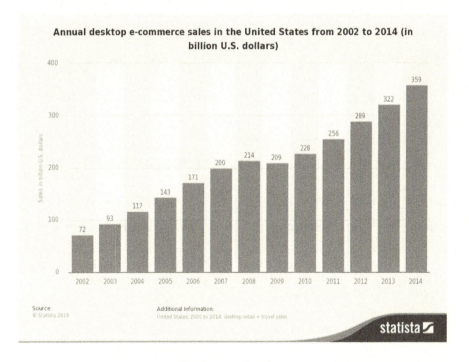

Annual desktop e-commerce sales in the United States from 2002 to 2014 (in billion U.S. dollars)

*Reference: Statista*

This is chart that shows how many desktop computers were bought online over a period of 12 years from 2002 to 2014.

As you can see, it started at $72 billion in 2002, and grew every year, except for a slight dip in 2009 because of the economic crash. After that it was back to a steady growth pattern reaching $359 billion in 2014. That's three hundred fifty-nine billion.

Now, imagine if we include laptops, smart phones and tablet sales.

The number will be enormous.

In 2017 researchers state that e-commerce sales will be 440.4 billion.

You might tell me "Oh this number is too big I have no idea."

You are not alone. Let me explain it to you this way.

Picture Bill Gates. Yes that Bill Gates, the Microsoft Bill Gates, the richest person in the world. What is a Bill Gates worth?

His estimated net worth in 2016 was $90 billion. In other words, e-commerce sales in

2017 will be equal to almost 5 Bill Gates! 5 BG.

Retail ecommerce sales in North America alone will $423.34 billion, maintaining the area's status as the world's second largest regional ecommerce market.

Now this next chart shows global e-commerce sales projecting into the future with an estimate of 1.5 trillion in 2018.

That's 18 times more than Bill Gates' net worth or 18 + BGs

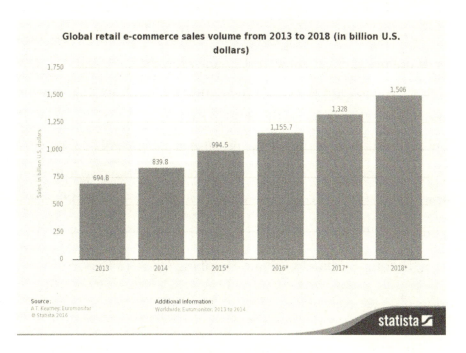

*Reference: Statista*

This indicates that physical retails stores will probably disappear one day.

Warren Buffett recently dumped his stock in Wal-Mart in favor of an investment in Amazon. Follow the leader.

So, if you want to run a profitable business, you have to get online. Yes you can still open a physical retail store, but you have to sell online as well. Otherwise your physical store will be gone no matter how big it is. Just like Sports Chalet, Sears, JC Penny, those big franchised stores we used to see in the shopping center.

## Numbers talk

Let me share a little fact with you. 69% of Americans buy stuff online, and 33% buy stuff online on a weekly basis. And the average transaction is $114.* The number is just gonna get bigger and bigger. I believe most of you have had the experience of buying stuff online, not only because it's convenient, but also because there's a lot of stuff you cannot find in the physical retail stores. Instead of spending money online, you should make money online. Don't you agree?

*(Resource: Mintel's Online Shopping US 2015 Report)

## E-commerce was....

The early stage of e-commerce was eBay online auctions. For me, I felt like online auctions were for people selling second hand products, who just make a little bit of additional income here and there.

## E-commerce is....

Today, e-commerce is an economic trend. E-commerce entrepreneurship makes it possible for tons of people to become self-made multi millionaires.

Basically, e-commerce is....

You buy **products** –at a lower cost from your **vendors**, and you **resell** these products by listing them ONLINE.

You sell the products at higher price, making profit on the difference between the cost and the retail price (this part is just like traditional business, just operating on a different platform).

And then you ship the products to end consumers – this is called fulfillment.

I'll provide you with more details about these things later, but as part of your e-commerce overview I want to introduce you to the Long Tail Strategy. This theory was first introduced in Wired Magazine by Chris Anderson in 2004. Why is it called Long Tail? As you can see in this chart, it looks like a long tail of an animal.

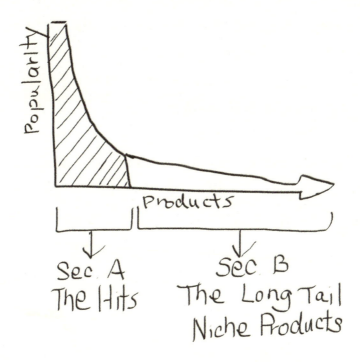

Please see the above diagram, Section A is the "hits" - the popular. And Section B is the "non-hits - niche product. There are not many popular products, but most of them have high demand. And there are a lot of different niche products, each one of them has low demand, but if you combine all of the niche products together, the demand is higher than the hits. So, after taking a quick glance, doesn't everyone want to do Section A?

If so, please say Section A out loud. Most people fail, because again, the hits, the red parts means lots of competition because everyone wants to do the red part. And the yellow part, not many people want to do it, so there's much less competition. Therefore it's easier to sell your niche products.

In the early stage of Amazon.com, when they used to sell only books, they were already using this long tail strategy. Imagine the Section A in the diagram represents Barnes & Nobles, they only sell popular books, so they have only 100 titles. This is just an example, not the real number. Section B in the diagram represents Amazon.com, they mostly sell unique books, and they sell 500 titles. Even though the demand is not high for each title, but most of them have buyers. So Amazon.com sells better than Barnes & Noble.

If you can understand the theory and apply it, this will be the key to your success.

## Ground Rules:

Let me tell you the ground rules for e-commerce.

First, this is not a get rich quick thing. That does not exist anywhere. If it did, everyone would be rich now.

Second, there's also no "do nothing, make tons of money." Especially when you first launch your business, you will need to spend a lot of time figuring out how everything works. Maybe, after the business is stable, you can work less, but it's impossible to do nothing at all.

If you think there's a job that can help you get rich over night by doing nothing, please email me because I would like to know.

Don't tell me about the lottery, the chances of winning are too small.

Now you have a picture of how big e-commerce is and where it came from – next is to figure out your place in this world. There are actually many ways to do e-commerce: drop-shipping, retail arbitrage, and private labeling. It can be mind-boggling. I'm going to talk about private labeling because that's the method that made my online store a 7-figure success.

**Q:** What is Private Labeling?

**A:** You buy existing products from manufactures directly, and re-sell them as your own brand.

If you want to learn about other e-commerce methods, I've included a BONUS information on my website since I don't want to go off topic from this book, below is the URL:

**ellenpro.com/gift/**

(Look for Chapter 3 Bonus: 4 Ways To Make Selling Online Work for you)

## Fulfillment options -

If you don't want to fulfill the products yourself, you can ship the products to Amazon fulfillment centers (Amazon FBA). That means, you pay Amazon warehouse for them to stock inventory and fulfill your products to end consumers. That way you don't have to worry about if you need a warehouse nor employees. You can also keep your day job by doing this on the side. Or you can even quit your job and fully focus on your online business.

**Q:** "I have a full time job, so I can't take care of the fulfillment myself, but Amazon FBA is too expensive for me, is there any alternative way to do this?"

**A:** "You can definitely consider those third party fulfillment centers because they are getting competitive, so they will definitely offer a more competitive price than Amazon FBA. But bear in mind that Amazon FBA will help your product ranking in Amazon.

Besides the Amazon fulfillment center, there are a lot of third party fulfillment centers out there now. These fulfillment centers were originally shipping forwarder companies. Because the logistics industry was not doing well, they converted themselves into fulfillment centers since they already had warehouses. And this was also a good opportunity for them to serve online sellers.

Next we are going to talk about how you can find the products that will make you money.

# CHAPTER 4

# Product, Price – Profit

After you understand the game of money from Chapter 2, you might ask me

"So exactly how do I build a profitable online store?"

## Start with the 4Ps

If you've studied about business before you probably know about the 4Ps:

Product, Price, Promotion, and Place.

It's what to sell, how much you sell, where to sell, and how to sell. These 4 elements are equally important. You need to have all of them to make your online business profitable long term. And these 4Ps determine whether you can make money online or not.

90% of the online sellers failed because they only had 2 or 3 Ps. And this 4P approach is exactly how I built my million dollar online business.

In this chapter I'm going to talk about Product and Price and how to figure out where the Profit will be.

## Product

Here's my biggest piece of advice, which may sound like the opposite of what you think.

**Don't: Sell popular products.**

**Do this: Sell niche products.**

Most people believe they have to sell popular products if they sell online. Because popular means high demand and high demand means money. And just because everybody does think that way, there are tons of people selling popular products.

So how can you compete with them? Lower your price?

The problem is that after you have lowered your price several times, your profit became smaller and smaller until it disappears. At the end, you will probably be losing money if you sell a unit just to beat your competitor's price.

Now how many of us have had this experience before? I did.

But, there are still some people who built a profitable business by selling popular products, however they spent thousands or ten thousands of money each month on advertising.

As a startup, selling popular products is going to be difficult for you if you don't spend thousands or ten thousands dollars each month on advertising, such as Facebook ads or Amazon pay-per-click.

You need to do this instead, you need to sell a niche product line with a lower demand.

I know that sounds backwards but here's why. Because you don't have as many competitors, your products can sell themselves - because they have niche value.

Without any advertising, without product reviews, you can still sell fast.

I have a student in my program, she found a niche product, and listed it on Amazon. She even forgot to add the keywords. The product started selling right away on the next day. And she's out of stock after a few weeks. So she tried again on another niche product she found, bought more inventory this time. And voila! It started selling right away the next day. She sold 4 units on the 2nd day, and more and more each day.

She told me "Selling a niche product is so easy, all I need to do is to put a label on it and send it to Amazon FBA. No need to do packaging, no need to work on reviews, pay-per-click, nor promotions like I used to do when I was selling popular products. This is amazing!"

## Picking your product – the rules

1. The retail price needs to be lower than $50, because this is the no-brainer price range people would purchase.

2. The product size needs to be smaller than that one-gallon milk jug you see in supermarket.

3. Also the package weight needs to be lighter than 2 pounds, so your product won't take too much of the space, and the shipping won't be that expensive.

4. And most importantly, you gotta have a lot of accessories to go with the product.

It's funny – once I made sure I had niche products that people actually wanted to buy (and were HAPPY that I carried these products), all the stuff I used to worry about fell right into place.

Because once I had some real money coming in, I could just pay to quickly solve problems that I used to spend months on.

Although I had discovered that I needed to prove demand for my idea for selling niche products, it wasn't enough to KNOW this concept. I had to figure out HOW to accomplish. How could I always find profitable niche products before selling them?

I decided to try a few things. I tried selling a few different product categories. I took different classes here and there. I read tons of entrepreneurial books and countless articles and researches. I talked to both successful online sellers and struggling online sellers. I even attended expensive conferences. Again and again, I heard the same concepts.

Over time, I combined these ideas into what I've found this single most effective way to determine if your products will sell well online- and let you hit 100K or more in revenue.

## Picking your product – the method

I call it the "Tab Tab Tab" Strategy. Thanks to this technique, I never have to wonder whether a product will sell well or not.

## How to find a profitable niche idea in 10-30 minutes:

**Step 1:** Gather all your product ideas. Here's how:

Get a piece of paper. Write down a list (at least 10) of potential product ideas based on you or your friends' hobbies. Check out Amazon's categories page if you need a prompt to get you started.

Cross out any product ideas that are fashion-related, cell phone-related, electronics-related, trendy products, and intangible items.

**Step 2:** Finish up with The Tab Tab Tab Strategy.

Watch this 10 minute video and follow the step-by-step instructions.

Here's the link: http://ellenpro.com/gift01

(I charge people for this course but you're getting this for free as a bonus from this book)

That's all there is to it! Within 30 minutes or less you can find ULTIMATE profitable products to sell online before you actually sell them. It's worked for me, and it can work for you!

It also worked for Dr. Young, a dentist friend of mine. You can see his story at http://ellenpro.com/tag/dentist/

## How to find vendors/suppliers –

Now that you've found your first profitable product idea, where are you going to get your product?

*Source From Asia*

Most of the online sellers source from Alibaba.com or aliexpress.com to import products mostly from China. You can also attend trade shows in China if you like to travel. To my best knowledge, the biggest trade show in China is Canon Fair in Guangzhou China.

*Source Locally*

If you want to find local vendors, you can check wholesalecentral.com or you can simply just Google it. Actually, some of the local vendors offer good pricing. You can also attend local trade shows to find local vendors.

*Become a distributor*

Or, if you already have a business, you can apply to become distributor of famous brands. But there are many restrictions for selling as a distributor, so you won't make much profit from it.

*Make your own products*

If you like to hand make stuff, you can build your own unique products.

**Do this: Sell your own brand with whole line, the more products the better**

**Don't: Sell only a few products**

A lot of people, sell only a few products, and over-focus on these few products.

They do giveaways for product reviews. And they got so crazy whenever someone steals their buy box.

Remember what I told you about the long tail strategy?

You gotta have your own brand - private-label it.

AND

You gotta have lots of different products.

The more products you have, the more traffic you get, the more exposure you have, and the more sales you will make. Look at those famous brands out there, which brand only carries one or two products? None of them. They all have a product line.

Let's take Apple for example. They sell computers with different specifications, and they sell Apple TV, IPhone, iPad, Apple Watch. It's a product line because they offer different specs. With the iPhone, you can choose from different colors, different memory storage sizes, and different phone sizes.

Let me tell you a story of one of my father's clients. We had this rich client who lived on a private island. He asked us to develop a new product for his company. He hired a super expensive French designer to design the product, spent tons of money on advertisement. But he still couldn't make this company profitable. After 2 years he finally found out the reason.

It was because his company only had one product. He finally realized this. He fixed this problem by developing a whole product line. And finally started generating profits.

I've been asked - Doesn't it take a lot of money to build a product and brand it with logo printing on the product and package? This is what people are used to seeing in retail store.

But you don't have to do all that in an online store. As long as the product is not patented nor branded already, you can technically buy anything and resell it as your own brand. For example, if you buy a cup at 99 cents store, and there's no logo on this cup, and the design is not patented - you can resell this cup online.

Just add your brand name in the product title online. So you can put "Ellenpro Brown Cup" something like that, then this cup becomes your product. Cup is obviously not a niche product, but works as a quick example of how easy it can be.

## Inventory, SKUs, UPC -

When you have lots of products, lots of SKUs you will have inventory control problems.

So I got this question from a guy - He asked me

"How do I do inventory control?"

The answer is - You need inventory software.

And you need to have UPC barcodes on each unit.

Step 1: Buy UPC codes (digital) from eBay or other websites that sell UPC.

Step 2: Use a UPC code generator and generate the code in a printed format

Step 3: Buy adhesive stickers online

Step 4: Put the sticker on each unit

Step 5: Setup the UPC code to associate with the product in the inventory software

Step 5: Scan the UPC code on the unit when it's shipped

Step 6: The inventory system will deduct the quantity from your inventory software.

**What To Sell?**

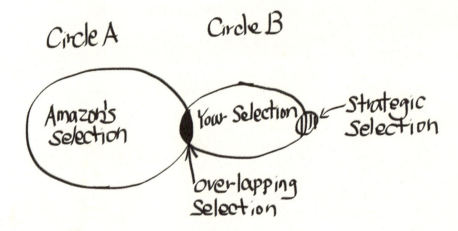

In the above picture, Circle A on the left is *Amazon's Product Selection* - the products that already exist in Amazon Prime.

Circle B on the right is *Your Product Selection* - your own brand, unique non-strategic product selection.

The *Overlapping Product Selection* in the middle - is what you will need to carry that's already on Amazon, basically products of other people's brands, especially the famous brands. That will increase your traffic to your store.

On the very right hand side, *Strategic Product Selection* - this will be your biggest secret weapon; basically it's the customized products that other people don't offer. You don't need to have too many of those, but you must have them. And <u>most of your sales</u> come from this part.

Sounds good?

Next I'm going to talk about how to carry more products with minimum budget.

**Do this:** Buy 20-30+ SKU (types of products) at once, 10-20 units per SKU, buy more when it sells well

**Don't do this:** Buy a few hundred of units per SKU to reduce the cost without testing the water.

Most online sellers don't test the market. They buy hundreds or thousands of units of one product at the very beginning. They reason that they want to get a lower cost-per-unit price or are caught in matching the minimum order quantity.

And then what happens? They have invested all of their money on this one particular product and the product sells really, really slowly. They end up with no money left to invest in new products.

These people would tell me, "I'll invest in new products when I sell out everything."

And then what happened? They kept lowering the price but it was still difficult to sell and they barely made any profit.

How many of you have experienced this?

What you need to do instead is buy 20-30 different products and get 20 units of each product, to test the market. If any of them sells fast, next time you can buy more than 100 units to reduce the cost. For the products that don't sell very well, just discontinue them.

By doing this you will maximize your investment and minimize the risk.

How much is the initial investment?

It really depends on you. For example if the product cost is $3 per unit and you buy 20 units of 10 different products plus transportation - it's about $600-$700.

Or if you only want to buy one product with 10 units that's under $100.

I want to emphasize as strongly as possible the importance of experimenting. No matter what you do, buying products or buying advertisement, you gotta be testing all the time.

Experiment, experiment, non-stop experiment until you find the one that works.

## A List of Product Ideas

Because the online market is constantly changing, I can't list the best product ideas here (it would probably be outdated by the time you read this book.) So I provide you with a digital version that I am constantly updating.

Download a list of profitable product ideas to start sourcing and selling now: **ellenpro.com/gift/**

I usually charge a couple of hundred dollars for the product list, but I'm giving you the top 5 from the list for free since you are taking your time to read this book, so go download the list now.

(Look for Chapter 4 Bonuses: The Top 5 Product Ideas for E-Commerce Ventures)

## The Second P is Price

The second P is the price. Most of the people don't do research on their competitor's price, and end up setting their retail price too high. Your potential buyers will compare and go to your competitors who are offering a lower price.

**Do this:** Check your top 3 competitors' prices every month, offer the lower price if possible.

**Don't:** Set your prices without checking competitor's prices

Researchers have found that 94% of the buyers will take time to find the lower price product online.

You might think your product has better quality, so you go with deluxe pricing. But, since you're not an international brand yet - you're not Chanel, you're not BMW - your brand name doesn't mean luxury to your potential buyers yet and they will probably be unwilling to pay you a premium price. But, you <u>will</u> be able to adjust your price upward after your brand name becomes a top seller in your category.

**Do this:** Calculate: Your retail price – Marketplace fee – Product Cost > Product Cost- Marketplace Fee = Profit

*Marketplace fee is the commission that marketplace charges whenever you sell an item.*

*It's usually 15% of the retail price.*

**Don't:** Set lowest prices for your products without checking other fees.

Some people offer the lowest price without checking to see if it's profitable or not - and end up losing money. When you set your price, please follow this rule. Your retail price minus cost minus shipping fee needs to be greater than your product cost – this is where your profit lies.

Once I discovered this, I didn't just say, GREAT and go crazy, I went to my market.

I tested it. Once. Twice. Three Times. And it worked!

Let me share some results:

Finding and selling a new niche product line, I secured $200,000 sales in just one month!

The best part was that I could determine if a product would sell well BEFORE I purchased them.

And it worked for everyone else who has tested it too.

Daniel followed the instructions in The Tab Tab Tab Strategy and got a GREAT profitable product idea after 10 minutes. He literally just decided what he could sell right after he watched the video for The Tab Tab Tab Strategy.

Jake avoided months of wasted effort when he found out his products would never work- and went on to sell something better.

That's the power of validating your product idea FIRST.

If you want to learn how to leverage the 4Ps to kick off your e-commerce business, I've included a bonus on my website: a step-by-step PDF for you to download, so you can print it out and hang it on your wall. Below is the URL: **ellenpro.com/gift/**

(Look for Chapter 4 Bonuses: How to Leverage the 4P's to Kick Off Your Online Business)

# CHAPTER 5

# Your Marketplaces and Your Web Store

## The 4th P is Place

Where you are going to sell you products online.

**Don't**: Rely on one marketplace

**Do this:** List your products in multiple marketplaces, to increase product/brand exposure.

Most online sellers only care about Amazon, like Amazon is the only way to sell, and they make the mistake of ignoring all other marketplaces. Think about this. If your products sell well on Amazon AND if you also sell on eBay, you get additional revenue. That's simple.

Now, here's something that most people don't realize. Based on my experiments I discovered that some products might become top sellers on eBay, but not Amazon. It's not because the customers are so different but because their algorithms are different.

You should see Amazon or eBay as one of your selling platforms, not the only one.

I chatted with many successful online sellers at a conference in Las Vegas. They all said that they sell on multiple marketplaces.

What you need to do is list your products on multiple marketplaces, getting more product and brand exposure.

You probably think it will take a lot of time to do that, right?

That's why you need an automated software package to do it for you. In the software you create a listing once, and then it will send the listing information to multiple marketplaces or channels at once. There are more than 10 software companies who can do that for you. Simply do a Google search for "Multi-Channel listing software."

Fantastic, right? And so easy once you know about it.

Since the online software market changes rapidly, I've included the most updated "Multi-Channel listing software on my website for you: ellenpro.com/gift/

(Look for Chapter 5 Bonus: The Complete List of Multichannel Listing Software)

Let me tell you the revenue ratios from different marketplaces for my company.

Amazon USA is only 39%. Think about it. If I could sell $10,000 per month on Amazon, then by listing in multiple marketplaces, my total monthly sales could turn into $25,641.

If you don't want to list on all of them, that's okay too.

I can tell you my top 3 marketplaces are eBay, Amazon, Walmart.

## You can easily be an international company

**Don't**: Only sell domestically

**Do this:** Sell on foreign marketplaces

Most sellers list their products only on domestic marketplaces.

They miss out on huge revenue from foreign buyers in foreign marketplaces.

I had a neighbor who worked next door to our warehouse.

They were also doing online selling and they asked me,

"Don't you think sales are slow this year?"

I told him "No, actually our sales is better than last year."

He looked concerned so I asked,

"Do you guys sell your products to foreign countries?"

He said "No," and asked, "Why would people in the foreign countries want to buy our products? The shipping fee is quite expensive."

And I answered, "Some of countries don't have enough resources, maybe they cannot buy the products you can sell to them. And sometimes the price you can offer from here plus a shipping fee is cheaper than what they could get in their own countries."

## What about selling in different languages?

They do use different languages in many foreign countries. But think about this.

How many other places in this world also use English? USA, Canada, Australia,

New Zealand and UK for starters. That's a lot of buyers. These marketplaces allow foreign sellers. So you should take advantage of this. Also be aware that Amazon UK attracts buyers from its surrounding countries, such as France, Spain, Germany and Italy.

Multiple marketplaces mean multiple sources of income streams. The more income streams you have, the more revenue you get. Of course, it will take a lot of time if you list all your products manually per marketplace. That's why you need a multi channel listing software.

Let me sum up. The following steps work for any products, any marketplaces, and any countries.

**Step 1: Find a niche product line, private label it (your own brand, find supplies from alibaba.com or other sourcing websites (test your products, so don't order hundreds of units per product for your first batch)**

I recommend starting from one niche product line, so buyers will think you're a specialized store and keep buying from you. You can find supplies from aliabba.com or local vendors. For the beginning, just get 20-30 units per each product to test the market.

**Step 2: Offer the lowest price of all domestic sellers. (Make sure it's still profitable)**

No need to care about the selling prices for Chinese sellers as there is no way you can compete with them on price. But that's okay, you may be able to compete on delivery time - remember many buyers don't want to wait for 3-4 weeks delivery.

**Step 3: List your products in multi marketplaces. Go international, such as eBay, Jet, Amazon Canada/UK/US, and etc.**

**Step 4: Build a web store, get on social media, build brand perception.**

**Step 5: On a regular basis, repeat step 1, keep looking for new products to sell to scale your business.**

This is the step to grow your company and brand perception. The faster you get to repeat this step, the faster your company scales up.

## Marketplaces

Think of each marketplace like you think of multiple streams of revenue.

You can't just have one. You need to have as many as possible.

## Amazon.com

Amazon is the biggest marketplace now, and I believe it will continue to be the biggest for many years. So yes, Amazon is the first marketplace you need to get on.

However since it's the biggest marketplace with more than 2 million sellers worldwide.

How can you get your products to stand out? There are a several ways:

### Niche Products Drive Organic Traffic:

We talked about this in the previous chapter, selling niche categories, so you have fewer competitors. Whenever a potential customer searches in Amazon, your products will automatically show up in the first few pages because there are not many sellers carrying the product. This is organic traffic.

## Advertising via Amazon PPC (Pay-Per-Click):

This is probably the quickest way to get going and works best if you're selling products with many competitors. You buy advertisement for a fee from Amazon, and Amazon will show your products on the first page of a search as "Sponsored Products"

## Optimized Keywords:

Make sure your product title and your product keywords are something that people actually search for it. Think from a buyer's perspective instead of seller's perspective. Try entering a keyword in the Amazon search box, and Amazon will automatically populate the keywords that most people search for. (See below photo)

## Use FBA service (Fulfilled By Amazon):

Have you ever wonder how to get the "Prime" logo on your products?

You need to join the FBA program, get Amazon to stock inventory and fulfill the products for you. By doing this, you get the following benefits:

1. You don't need to fulfill the products yourself

2. You don't need to have a warehouse to stock the inventory

3. Buyers will be able to find your products more easily than non-Prime products,

This is how Amazon's searching algorithm works. Be aware that there are more than 54 million Prime members on Amazon, a lot of them look for only "Prime" products to take advantage of free Prime shipping.

## Product Reviews:

You don't need a lot of reviews, 3-5 reviews is good to start with. It's not that difficult to get 3-5 reviews, right? Just ask your friends to buy and write a nice review for you.

Use your network.

Go International via Amazon platforms:

Besides Amazon USA, there is Amazon Canada, Amazon Mexico, Amazon Japan,

Amazon India, Amazon UK, Amazon Italy, Amazon Germany, Amazon Spain,

Amazon France, and many more.

This is the fastest way to build an international brand, to be seen by the world.

And Amazon has already built that platform for you.

Get your products there first!

## eBay.com

Although everyone talks about Amazon, eBay still has a huge international market.

The search algorithm for eBay is pretty simple. It's all about keywords. The more relevant keywords you put in there, the more likely your product can be found by potential buyers. Again, think from buyer's perspective and use eBay's search bar to find the most popular keywords people search for.

*Setting price:* Because there's a search filter "Price + Shipping: Lowest First" in eBay, price matters in eBay a lot. Make sure you offer competitive price + free shipping. As I said before, you can't compete with the incredible low price offered by sellers in

Asia, but you may be able to compete on delivery. Because some people don't like to wait for 3-4 weeks for their product to arrive.

*Enroll in Global Shipping Program:* With just a few simple clicks inside your account settings, your products can be found in all eBay platforms, this includes: eBay USA, eBay Canada, eBay Germany, eBay France, eBay Spain, eBay Italy, eBay Netherlands, eBay Ireland, eBay Australia, eBay Singapore, eBay Hong Kong, eBay Austria, eBay Switzerland.

## Walmart.com

Besides the products you see inside of your local brick and mortar Walmart store, did you know Walmart also has a marketplace like Amazon.com? The challenge is that they only take companies who hit certain level of revenue. But if you can get into the Walmart marketplace, you will make good money there.

## Jet.com

Jet is a fairly new company founded in 2014, but acquired by Walmart in 2016 for $3 billion. They have a unique paying system, with the slogan "Prices Drop As You Shop."

You can pay less if you select different payment/return option (as shown in the below picture)

| | | |
|---|---|---|
| ⦿ **$54.98** | Starting price | |
| ○ **$54.39** | If you opt out of free returns on this item, you pay less. | Details |
| ○ **$54.54** | If you pay by debit card, you pay less. | Details |
| ○ **$53.95** | If you opt out of free returns on this item and pay by debit card, you pay less. | Details |

| No Thanks | Update Cart |
|---|---|

Also, the more units you buy, the less money you pay. So they focus on how much customers save by doing this and that. As a seller, you don't have to worry about how that works, Jet calculates everything on its end.

## Etsy.com

If you're selling fashion or handmade products, this is the marketplace you need to get on.

## ASOS.com

ASOS is a UK fashion-shopping site, but they also have a marketplace available for sellers.

If you're selling fashion related products, you should get on ASOS.com!

## Newegg.com

Newegg is well known for electronics, so if you are selling electronics, you should sell on their marketplace. However they also allow their sellers to sell non-electronic related products on their marketplace. Worth checking out.

## Rakuten.com

Previously known as Buy.com, it was purchased by the Japanese company Rakuten in 2010.

## Sears.com

Sears also has its own marketplace like Walmart.com. You can simply apply to become a marketplace seller and start selling on the Sears marketplace.

## TradeMe.com

TradeMe.com's target audience is only New Zealand, but if you're selling something that people in New Zealand might like it, you should get on TradeMe.com

## MercadoLibre.com

MercadoLibre is the biggest marketplace in South America. If you're selling products that can appeal to South Americans, you should get on MercadoLibre.

## Lazada.com

Originally founded by a German company, Lazada is the biggest marketplace in Southeast Asia. It covers Indonesia, Thailand, Vietnam, Singapore, and Malaysia, and Philippines. They have a unique paying system and buyers don't pay until they receive the orders.

# CHAPTER 6

# Build Your Place in the Market with Promotion and Social Media

Your web store is your place in the e-commerce market. It is an appreciating asset that you can build on for success. It lives and grows on promotion.

Here's how to start.

You can simply and easily get your web store started by using Shopify or Bigcommerce.

They provide pretty built-in templates you can use. You don't have to spend big bucks hiring web developers.

Most online sellers focus only on Amazon and ignore their own web store.

But, you know what you can do with your web store? You can use it to collect buyer's emails.

Then you send them weekly newsletters. You tell them about promotions. This drives sales to your site. A newsletter is the single most effective way to communicate with all your customers at once, and make them become returning customers.

I used this method, and collected 26,000 emails in 5 years. And the customer return rate is 25%. Which means, one out of 4 customers became our loyal customer.

You may also bring these customers to your Amazon store, but don't forget that Amazon charges you 15% commission. So think about this, if you can offer a 10% off coupon and bring the customers to your web store, it will motivate them to buy more. And you're actually making more profit because you skipped Amazon's 15% commission.

But don't think having a web store only is good enough. Plenty of folks out there will tell you that you only need Shopify and Facebook Ads or Google Ads. A friend of mine was selling online and they only had a web store. They ended up spending $5000 per month on Google advertisements. After a half-year, they shut down their business because they didn't have any more money.

Altogether they spent $30,000 on advertisement. That's $30,000 for Google but no result for their web store. They thought advertising would bring revenue. How many of you believed this too? I believed it as well, but it turned out it's not true. That's because it takes you so much time and investment to boost up the traffic on your web store. So, you should see your web store as just one of your income platforms.

## A Simple Secret

People ask me how to get more people to go to their web stores. The simplest answer is to go to this website called similarweb.com, and enter your competitor's web address in there. You will see where their traffic comes from and you will know where your potential customers are.

Just do the same thing as your competitors do.

**Don't:** Ignore social media platforms.

**Do this:** Promote or post interesting stuff on social media platforms on a regular basis.

And let's talk about social media platforms such as Facebook, Twitter, Instagram, and YouTube.

The purpose of social media works like free advertisement. By regularly posting about your brand, you let more people know about you, so you establish your brand perception. After they know about your product and brand, by seeing regular posts over time, one will grab their attention and maybe they will think about purchasing. You can post a Facebook ad to link to your website, and ask them to purchase right away. But what you really want to do with a Facebook Ad is to bring people to your fan page, or another landing page to collect their emails. Then you can e-mail market to them.

Social media is crucial at the early stage your business. Many potential buyers rely on the number of your followers to decide if they want to buy from you. For example, if you saw a Facebook Ad today and this ad is linked to a website that you have never seen before you might wonder: Is it safe? Are the products genuine? You would probably Google the company name or check out their Facebook page.

If you see a company with thousands of followers, you would conclude that this company is legit. So the whole purpose of social media platform is building your brand perception. It's also how to build a brand fast.

You can do one other thing in social media... Find an influencer on Instagram or Facebook. This person needs to have thousands or ten thousands of followers and be regularly posting about something that's related to your products. You can pay this person, send your product to them, and ask them to promote your product on their social media platform.

Here's another question I was asked -

**Q:** What if I'm promoting something that's completely new in the US, and nobody knows about this, how could a potential customer search for this product?

**A:** In this case, your best bet is to find out any related keywords for this product, and also to use the power of social media influencers, let them promote your product and spread the news for you.

It's most difficult to generate traffic to your web store when you first launch it. Launch time is when you need to work the hardest to create traffic. If you ask me what's the most effective way? I would say test all of them and see which ones work for your business.

Below I'm going to talk about the many different ways to do it.

- Google Adwords

  Buy keywords on google.com and have your website pop out on the first page of the search result

- SEO (Search Engine Optimization)

  Write better keywords in your website to get organic search (without paid advertisement), this includes writing blogs under the domain of your web store.

- E-Mail Marketing

  Collect emails for those who visited your websites, send them weekly newsletters to encourage them to buy.

- Affiliated Marketing

  Set up an affiliated program for your site, offer a commission to affiliate marketers whenever someone purchase from your site by clicking their affiliated link. Most of the major marketplaces have affiliated program, so you should do this too. You can list your site on affiliated marketplaces.

• Influencer Marketing

Pay an influencer to promote your products on their own channels, or you can give them commission for each unit sold.

• Media Advertisement

Buying advertisement on the top website of your industry

• Re-Marketing

• Once a potential buyer visits your website, they will see your ad follows them everywhere, in Facebook, in major news website, etc.

• Social Media Marketing

If you're not on social media, you don't live in 21st century. In the next chapter, I will break down the details with each social media platforms.

Social media is the trend. A lot of businesses have been built just by getting the leads from social media platforms. There are tons of books out there about social media. I'm just going to cover some of the basics, so you will understand what social media platforms are good for starting your e-commerce business.

## Facebook

Definitely the top social media platform is Facebook! And the most effective way to reach people is to buy Facebook Ads; I would just set a budget of $5 per day to run some tests.

In order to run an ad on Facebook, you need to create a fan page.

The best part? Thanks to Mark Zuckerberg, you can also have your ad show on Instagram and other affiliated sites when you purchase an ad from Facebook.

How to create an effective Facebook ad: Break it down into 3 sections:

*Audience set-* always test different audience sets until you find the one that converts the best!

*Ad Picture -* This will be your product photo!

*Ad text-* Coupon deals works the best in Facebook ads for e-commerce. Add emojis in there to get people's attention!

## Instagram

Instagram is in second place for social media. Because of the use of hashtags, you can pretty much reach out to tons of people out there who are interested in your topic. So make sure you use a lot of hashtags! What you can also do in Instagram is reach out to influencers and have them promote your products for a commission or fee.

For example, if you're selling culinary products, you can simply search #culinary, #kitchenware, or #cooking in Instagram to find those people who are interested in their topic. And check their follower number to determine if they're influencers (influencers usually have 10K+ followers)

## YouTube

People go to YouTube all the time for the "how-to" videos. So if you upload some videos for some "how-tos" with your products, it will bring traffic. And you can also monetize your YouTube channels, that's another source of income stream for you. Here's how to optimize YouTube videos: Use the Video titles and Video descriptions. Make sure you enter lots of keywords in the video descriptions and link to other popular YouTube videos in the video description area)

## LinkedIn

This works more for B2B (Business to Business) selling, but what you can also do is to join various LinkedIn groups, and post something there. It will get people's attention. Also post on your LinkedIn timeline so your connections get notified.

## Pinterest

Works the best if you're selling fashion related products. People always go to Pinterest to get fashion ideas.

There are many more platforms that you can explore to gain more exposures. I created a video to talk about the strategies for each platform. You can find it here: ellenpro.com/gift/

(Look for Chapter 6 Bonus: Social Media Platforms to Build Brand Exposures)

As I mentioned before, the most efficient way to proceed is to have a central posting that feeds to others. Write one post, and use a hub that will automatically schedule posts onto multiple platforms all at once.

Consider the following:

- Buffer

- Hootsuite

- IFTTT (If This Then That)

# CHAPTER 7

## Formula for Success

Burning Desire
Mindset
+ Practical Strategies
_____
SUCCESS

First you need to find a burning desire.

Then with the proper mindset, it will lead you to the practical strategies and ultimately to success.

Frankly, most people don't have burning desires. They assume that they don't have control over what's happening to them in life. Don't worry, it takes time to find this burning desire. After you find it you need to envision all the details in your head and remind yourself of it every single day. You need to set this burning desire very high.

Why? For example, if you set a goal of making $10,000 per month, then you will make $10,000/mo. or less in the future. If you set a goal of making $100,000 per month, you will make

$100,000 or less per month in the future. That's why people say "Dream Big."

But you might ask me this - How can I achieve this goal, it looks impossible.

If you think it's impossible at the beginning, you will not make any changes, and then it is impossible. If you think you will need to achieve the goal no matter what, you will take time to learn how to get there, and start changing yourself, doing things differently.

If the goal is too small, so small that you don't need to change yourself, so small you don't need walk out from your comfort zone. Then this is not a burning desire. Now, do you have a burning desire yet?

## Burning Desire

"To achieve anything, you need a burning desire."

Napoleon Hill, author of the classic *Think and Grow Rich*

Motivational author and speaker, Tony Robbins, also talks about this burning desire all the time. This concept is called Law of Attraction. Whatever you want to do, you gotta think about it first in the head, and you gotta take action when opportunity knocks. If you don't take action, nothing will change, you won't be able to achieve any goals. I truly believe that everything I have today is all due to the law of attraction.

## Mindset

Let's talk about mindset now.

One of my friends asked me this before

"What exactly did you do to make your business successful?"

I told him "It's not really about what I did, it's about what's in my head, my mindset."

## Grow-Change-Learn

Like I mentioned earlier. Most of the small business owners got stuck because they spent most of their time maintaining their business. The Online world is very competitive, if your business doesn't grow, you will get outrun by growing competitors. You have to do something differently each year, really each quarter.

If you tell me your business is not going well because the economy is bad, I would ask if you have done anything differently every year to grow your business. If not, don't blame the economy, it was simply because you got outrun by your competitors. But, if you understand the formula, it's easy for you to outrun them.

Maybe you and your friends like to talk about investing in stocks. But let me tell you this.

What you need to invest in the most is not stock, it's yourself, your personal growth.

Not long ago, I met an elderly man. He loaned me a book and asked me to finish as soon as possible. I asked him how long does it take to finish this book? He told me about 10 hours.

I explained to him that I don't have that much time. He told me,

"A human is like a mold of a cup. The more knowledge you have, the bigger your mold is.

You will be able to put more in yourself, able to achieve more. If you don't change your mold size, what you can achieve today will be the same as what you could achieve yesterday.

Warren Buffett's partner Charlie Munger said this

"Spend each day trying to be a little wiser than you were when you woke up."

This quote stuck in my head. I hope I can get it stuck in your head as well.

## The second mindset is persistence.

Most people fail because they give up too soon.

However, it's not so much about persisting in your methods, it's about you persisting in your visions and goals. When you find a business idea, don't get beat up by challenges.

Persist in your vision, turn sideways and approach your goals in a different way.

Awhile back. Mark Zuckerberg hosted a Q&A session on Facebook. In this session you could ask him anything. So someone asked him "What your biggest secret for success?"

He simply replied "don't give up.

If you have read the book *Facebook Effect* or watched the movie *The Social Network*, you should know Mark encountered numerous challenges on his path. But he never gave up. He always found a way to make it work.

## The third mindset is dedication.

This is pretty straightforward. You need to enjoy your work, and oftentimes you forget about the time because you enjoy it so much. And you know your dedication will make a huge impact on your revenue. But don't overdo this. Most of the one-man entrepreneurs spent too much time at work, and forgot about the quality of life.

Entrepreneurships is not only about making more money, it's more about happiness and freedom. Tai Lopez says there are 4 pillars for success: Love, Wealth, Health, and Happiness. You need to balance these 4 pillars, use your time wisely.

## The last mindset is gratitude.

You gotta be grateful to your customers, they are the reason why you have sales.

You gotta be grateful to your employees - you cannot operate a company without their help.

And gratitude is contagious. If you express this feeling to them, they will most likely express the same to you. Your customers will become your loyal fans. This mindset can also apply in personal relationships including your family and friends. So those are the 4 basic mindsets.

## Procrastination is your biggest enemy

Many people understand they have to take time and effort to make a difference, but they keep procrastinating because they cannot find time to do the hard work. Even if they find time to do it, they don't feel like doing it. Success doesn't happen by just thinking about it, action is what it matters.

Let me ask you this. Do you have one hour per day you can use? This may be the one hour before you go to sleep, or the one hour after work. And what are you currently doing with this one hour? Are you watching TV or playing video games?

I've included a bonus video for you: "Time Management Tricks to Reach Even Greater Success." I use this technique to run two companies at the same time: ellenpro.com/gift/

(Look for Chapter 7 Bonus: Time Management Tricks To Reach Even Greater Success)

## Practical Strategies

Now let's talk about the last element of successful formula-practical strategies. This process takes the most time, because you need to keep experimenting different ways, and find out which works the best. And you have to invest in yourself when the opportunity knocks. Think about this, if you invest $1000 in yourself, you will make $10,000. Would you do this?

You can find many of these practical strategies from reading books, attending seminars and taking online classes. My mentor Matt Pocius once told me this

"Invest 20% of your net income on yourself for greater success."

OR

You can hire a mentor who has already reached your goal. I was amazed when I discovered that I could hire a mentor and it has proved to be invaluable in shortening my learning curve and speeding up my rise to success. You will have noticed by now that I refer often to my mentors.

I am not the only one who has benefitted by this help. Read on.

# CHAPTER 8

# The Power of Mentors

Do you realize how many successful entrepreneurs have had mentors behind them?

Steve Jobs was Mark Zuckerberg's mentor. Warren Buffett is Bill Gates' mentor.

Freddie Laker is Richard Branson's mentor.

Richard Branson once said this "It's always good to have a helping hand at the start.

I wouldn't have got anywhere in the airline industry without the mentorship of Sir Freddie

Laker. Now I love mentoring young entrepreneurs.

As American author and businessman Zig Ziglar said, "A lot of people have gone further than they thought they could because someone else thought they could.

For the most part of my life, my mentor was always my father. He has been an entrepreneur for more than 30 years. But after I studied books on entrepreneurship, I realized that I had to grow beyond his mindset of just maintaining a small business. In order to become something even bigger, I realized I needed to find new mentors.

First I met Jack Canfield, the co-author of the *Chicken Soup for Soul* series. Even if you never read these books you have probably heard of them. Starting with one book he has grown a publishing, consumer product and media company. What Jack told me was that everyone needs one or two mentors. And this mentor needs to be someone who already achieved the success that you want.

I met my first mentor Matt Pocius on Facebook in 2016. He was a 21-year-old young man from Lithuania. He was very young but very successful. Matt was featured in an article on Entrepreneur.com. They call him "The Youngest Highest Paid Internet Consultant in the world." His hourly rate is $4000 per hour. He made his first million when he was 18. So I hired him as my mentor.

There was this one time Matt came to Los Angeles, and he invited me to go this mastermind session at Tai Lopez's Beverly Hills mansion. That's how I found out Tai Lopez was actually Matt Pocious's mentor. I was actually in Tai's beginner's program a while back, but that was the first time I saw Tai in person. I will talk about what I learned from Tai Lopez quite often. He is known for his Ted Talk, and has more than 20 multi-million businesses. His entrepreneurial mindset is inspiring and he's frequently surrounded by other famous entrepreneurs, such as Mark Cuban. Tai throws a lot of parties at his mansion, and people who get invited are usually celebrities or multi-millionaires.

So that day, I met Keith Aichele in Tai's house. Keith is America's extreme Marketing expert. I talked to Keith at the party and he invited me to go his seminar. I ended up hiring him as my second mentor. At this point, I realized how important it is to network with people, especially awesome people. You have to leave your comfort zone, go out and see how big this world is with all the successful people.

Maybe you would feel a little bit uncomfortable at first, you might feel like you don't belong to the world of successful people. But after a while, everyone you meet will either be entrepreneurs, multi-millionaires, book authors, or public speakers. And you will start thinking, "How can I just be an ordinary person?" So you will start learning from these people, and make yourself become a part of the successful world.

And guess what? With the invaluable insight from my mentors, I skyrocketed my online coaching program after just 18 months in business. They also opened doors and took me into a different world that I had never seen before - a world full of successful like-minded entrepreneurs. I was able to meet Hollywood actresses, book authors, life coaches and public speakers. I even did a quick video with Lewis Howes when I attended the VIP Party after his seminar. As a FOB Taiwanese-American, I never saw this coming in my life.

# And now here I am

*With my first mentor Matt Pocius*

*My second mentor Keith Aichele and myself on stage*

*My public speaking mentor Christopher Kai*

## How To Pre-Qualify Your Mentors?

It's crucial to hire a mentor, but you don't just hire anyone. You will need to hire someone who's already achieved what you want to become. If you want to become a basketball player, you don't hire a baseball coach. If you want to become a 6-figure speaker, you don't just hire anyone who's been on the stage. If you want to become a 7-figure e-commerce shop owner, you hire someone who's already done it, not just anyone who's doing e-commerce.

Below is a list of questions you should ask when qualifying a mentor:

1. Is he/she an expert in the area you want to achieve?

2. Has he/she achieved the goal you want to achieve?

3. Can you reach out to him/her directly? (The reason I put this up is because there are many online courses out there you don't get to talk to the "experts" but their support team.)

Currently I have three mentors in three different areas. Keith Aichele is my marketing mentor, Matt Pocius is my coaching business mentor, and Christopher Kai is my public speaking mentor. And I will have more mentors in the future as I want to develop more skill sets.

So if you're serious about becoming a successful e-commerce entrepreneur, you should hire a 7-figure e-commerce mentor/coach who's been there and done that. I do have a coaching program available. You can get more information at ellenpro.com

## Ways To Find Mentors?

Want to know "3 Ways To Find Mentors To Make Millions"? I've included a bonus video on my website: ellenpro.com/gift/

(Look for Chapter 8 Bonus: 3 Ways to Find a Mentor to Make Millions)

# CHAPTER 9

# How to scale your business

Soon after you start your business you will start to think about how to make it bigger.

Before you start flinging yourself around trying different things – let's review the basics.

I have a simple strategy for you to learn. This strategy is called the "E-Commerce Pro Score"

Remember - there are two main elements to scale your e-commerce businesses:

Channels and Products.

**Channels:** These are your marketplaces.

More marketplaces = more selling channels

TIMES

**Products:** More SKUs. A long product line.

EQUALS

**E-Commerce Pro Score:**

Together these two elements multiply together to build your successful e-commerce business.

# Channels
# x Products
---
# E-Commerce Pro Score

So it works like this:

If you are selling on Amazon and your web store that's two channels.

Let's say you have 50 products. So let's do the math here:

2 x 50 = 100

100 is the health score of your e-commerce business. Obviously, the bigger the number the healthier your business will be.

Let's take my e-commerce business and plug into this calculation.

We have 14 channels (13 channels + one web store) and roughly around 3000 products.

14 x 3000 = 42,000

See the difference?

Plug your business into this calculation and see how much you get?

This should give you a better idea on what you should work on now. You can't have only one selling Channel (for example, just Amazon). Because what if Amazon decides to ban your account one day?

Lets' use my business again as an example (3,000 SKUs)

0 x 3,000 = 0

Lots of products, no channels.

You see, no matter how many products I have, I can't get any results by multiplying by 0.

1 x 3,000 =

That would be a dangerous business if I only sell on one channel.

Let's do another example, let's say you have only one product, and you are selling on 15 channels:

15 x 1 = 15

No matter how many marketplaces you list on, you can only score 15.

Think about this, what if your one product becomes outdated and nobody's gonna buy it after awhile? You get 0, no sales. That's also a very dangerous business.

In conclusion, always be prepared for your channels or products die. Because I'm telling you, it happens a lot. So what you need to do to scale your business is to build up as many channels and products as possible.

# CHAPTER 10

# Questions, Answers & Successes

I am honored to work with many entrepreneurs and I take pride when my advice helps them to succeed. Let me introduce you to a couple of them.

## Daniel from Canada

Daniel from Canada. A 9-5 employee of a big corporate. First time in e-commerce, he generated USD $47,164 in one month on Amazon USA, and USD$897 on Amazon Canada, USD $2,425.20 on Shopify, and USD$5,452 on eBay. The refund amount was $1,299. So He generated a total of USD $54,642 in just one month! And one of his products became Best Seller on Amazon Canada. And this was just a start. You know what? I believe he's going to become a millionaire pretty soon.

**Daniel** ˋ
Yesterday at 11:30 AM

I really want to thank **Ellen Lin**. One of my products has just hit No. 1 at an Amazon.ca's category. It is really amazing!

https://www.amazon.ca/gp/bestsellers                                     l/

| 17 others                                                    1 Comment

👍 Like                                    💬 Comment

## Mia from California

Mia from California. A small business owner of a wholesale company, successfully transitioned into e-commerce. Now she's making $4,601 in 7 DAYS!

## Rohit from India

Rohit had no experienced selling online, but he wanted to sell in USA. He was browsing online and he found other "so-called e-commerce experts," but they all talked about spending USD$5000+ to launch a business. He didn't have such a big budget so he decided to join our program because I'm known for starting my online business with only $600.

By joining our Million Dollar Golden Formula program, Rohit found his niche products within his budget and started selling online in USA from India.

## Sunny from California

Sunny launched her Amazon business in January 2016 with another Amazon instructor but later found out their program didn't work because she had to spend a lot of money on advertisement and Amazon PPC. She joined our program Million Dollar Golden Formula in May 2016, and finally was able to find niche products and sell on Amazon without spending a cent on ad.

## Louis from Illinois

Louis is an experienced online seller. He was always struggling with his sales. He signed up my coaching program for three weeks and he's already got a $5,000 increase in sales.

## Shelly from Texas

I'm was already selling online since 2008 but it never get to the level where I want it to be because I do everything on my own and don't have anyone to help me. Keeping the physical store afloat during the recession and taking care of kids and family seems too much to the point that I no longer wanted to keep store open but didn't have any exit plan at all. One day my husband received an email from Ellen and told me about it and at first I was very skeptical because I thought that it's for people that are just starting to sell online. But my husband paid for it so I said I'm going to check it out. And I was worried that my husband just wasted his money.

But it turns out…. The course helped me realized that there's a lot of things I don't know about selling online. Ellen was good in responding to my questions and I'm glad that I found a mentor. Million dollar Golden Formula helped me have that enthusiasm back and made me realized that I just can't give up on this dream and hoping that this is not just a "hobby" but I can turn it into a "real business" and that I can have the same level of success like Ellen's and others who made millions on the internet.

I realized the course was worth it when my sales on Amazon started picking up and the importance of using FBA to boost sales. Ellen also introduced me to using VA to speed up my work, which I didn't know existed until I signed up with her course.

Don't do it alone-you waste time money and precious time for family and the things you love to do. Use a mentor, the money you paid is all worth it.

There are a lot of stay-at-home moms that sacrifice their career to raise a family and they can still pursue their dream of owning a business like I do through selling online with help of this program.

## Gibril C. from UK

"Through your program I have made around $400 sales on Amazon, eBay and other platforms in December and January this year! Brilliant, thank you so much."

## Yvonne From California

Yvonne from California. Mom with 2 kids + 2 part time jobs. She generated $500/mo. in the 2nd month after enrolling in the program and after 7 months... Boom! $6,801.63 per month!

You can see more testimonials here:

**ellenpro.com/testimonials/**

## Getting Started – Is this something I can do?

**Q:** How can I get rid of my 9-5 job working for someone else?

**A:** Start an e-commerce business on the side, and once you are making more money on your e-commerce business you can quit your day job.

**Q:** I'd like to know for sure if this is something that can really be achieved by me or if it is something only a select few can do.

**A:** Every successful business takes hard work and the right strategies. But anyone can achieve this success with a willingness to work hard and the strategies I can offer.

**Q:** How can I make a million dollars in revenue?

**A:** Start small, and keep scaling by following the 4Ps (Chapters 4 and 5)

**Q:** What are the initial skills you need to start?

**A:** Basic computer skills are fine. You will learn as you go.

**Q:** What are the equipment requirements for starting an e-commerce business?

**A:** A computer with Wi-Fi

**Q:** How many employees are required to start an e-commerce business?

**A:** Just yourself.

**Q:** How and what type of online business can one start?

**A:** There are tons. You can sell services or physical products. They each have different approaches. For physical products, the quickest way is to get on marketplaces like eBay/Amazon.

**Q:** How to I start my first ecommerce business?

**A:** Just three steps:

Look for niche products 2. Source the products from aliababa.com 3. List them on eBay and Amazon marketplaces. Voila – you are in business.

**Q:** What is the best advice you can give to young entrepreneurs who are entering the business?

**A:** Taking action – just start!

**Q:** How to get approval to become Amazon seller?

**A:** Anyone can apply from Amazon.com

**Q:** How to sell on Amazon. What are the procedures?

**A:** First you create a listing, and send your products to Amazon FBA center.

https://services.amazon.com/fulfillment-by-amazon/how-it-works.htm

**Q:** What is the best strategy for marketing my brand on Amazon and eBay.

**A:** Carry a solid product line within the same category

**Q:** What if I want to sell handmade products online?

**A:** Get on etsy.com and promote through social media platforms

**Q:** Can I start an online business with limited money?

**A:** Yes, you can start with a small budget to buy products and immediately start selling them for profit

**Q:** How much is the cost to start up?

**A:** It depends on you, I would say a minimum of $500 – my father and I started with $600.

**Q:** How you do it with just $600?

**A:** Buy 20 SKUs, with 10 units each.

## Finding Products

**Q:** What kind of products can I sell to generate a good profit?

**A:** Start with the Tab Tab Tab Strategy as taught in Chapter 4 in this book. Use my online list and take my Million Dollar Golden Formula course.

ellenpro.com/course/million-dollar-golden-formula/

**Q:** What is the best place to locate products to sell on eBay and Amazon?

**A:** alibaba.com or aliexpress.com

**Q:** How to source goods directly from manufacturers at cheap price

**A:** Visit the manufacturers in person.

Q: How would I start if I have no money to buy products?

**A:** Sell your unwanted items at home on eBay to make money to invest your first batch of order.

**Q:** How to select the right goods putting on the rack.

**A:** By testing different products

## Pricing

**Q:** How to set the price for products?

**A:** Offer irresistible and competitive pricing (Do market research first)

**Q:** How to deal with a customer asked to lower a price and competition the price

**A:** If you really want the sales, match the price and sell to them. If you think it's not profitable, simply reject.

## Promotion

**Q:** How to increase traffic for my web store?

**A:** E-mail marketing + social media marketing + SEO + buy Facebook Ads.

**Q:** How to promote products and reach out to public without any fees (besides Facebook, etc.)

**A:** Marketplaces and other social media platforms such as Instagram.

**Q:** I would like to learn more about getting customer reviews on Amazon. If you are just starting up how do you get reviews?

**A:** You only need 3-5 reviews to get started, and you can get those from your family or friends.

**Q:** How to do business with eBay and Amazon?

**A:** You apply to become their sellers.

**Q:** How to acquire customers from competitors and stand out at the marketplace?

**A:** Study your competitors and sell what they don't have with the category.

**Q:** Are high costing products better to sell as opposed to low costing?

**A:** No, I recommend products under $50. But if your product is unique, it will sell as well.

## Marketplaces

**Q:** Which is best EBay, Letgo app or Craigslist?

**A:** Amazon and eBay are the two best now. Etsy for art and hand made goods.

**Q:** How can I quickly and easily post things on eBay?

**A:** By using a third party listing software. Just do a Google search for "multi-channel listing software."

**Q:** What are other marketplaces besides Amazon and eBay?

**A:** Check out Walmart.com and Jet.com, also Rakuten, Sears, Newegg, and a marketplace called TradeMe for New Zealand.

## Your Web Store

**Q:** What is the easiest way to get going with a website?

**A:** Shopify.com and Bigcommerce.com. both have templates for built-in shopping carts.

**Q:** How do I design my own web store?

**A:** You don't' have to design it. The easiest way is to use Shopify or Bigcommerce's service.

**Q:** What is Shopify?

**A:** Shopify is an e-commerce platform where you can build your web store with shopping cart.

The point of all your promotion and even your sales on the big marketplaces is to drive traffic and sales to your web store – this is where you will make the most money. (See Chapter 5)

## Improving Your Profits/Expanding your business

**Q:** How to grow audience?

**A:** Sell on multi marketplaces and get on all social media platforms.

**Q:** How can I make my online store better?

**A:** Use an appealing template so your website doesn't look like a SCAM.

Also make sure you collect people's emails by implementing a squeeze box.

*a pop-out window from your web store that collects people's email so you can do email marketing on them, below is an example:*

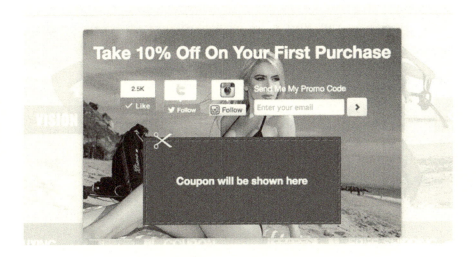

**Q:** How can I expand my small business when I only have full time and two part-time workers?

**A:** You can hire Virtual Assistants online.

**Q:** How to beat other competitors

**A:** Use the 4Ps to plan your strategy.

One of my followers said that he could not beat his competitor's price, so it's really difficult for him to make a sale. When I saw this question, I knew he's gotta be selling popular products. So, of course, it's a price war. Popular products mean more competitors, because everybody else wants to sell popular products.

I gave him 3 pieces of advice:

1. Change his product line,

2. See if he can find niche accessories in the same product category,

OR

3. Offer customized products. For example, let customers pick different colors on different parts of products like what Oakley sunglasses did on their website. He could also let customers add or remove elements. Another option is to offer something like name embroidery.

If you're willing to spend your time you can give your customer a different experience. Offer a service that others think it's time-consuming. In this way you can outrun everyone else.

**Q:** What if I have a product but no extra money for SEO, SEM or advertising – what can I do?

**A:** List on multiple marketplaces and utilize social media for free product exposure.

It is best to focus on one category of products so potential buyers will see you as a specialized store and keep returning to buy from you.

**Q:** How do you headline what you are selling? E.g. free shipping?

**A:** Free shipping is the norm now. So I wouldn't put that as a headline/title area. Make sure you enter as many keywords as possible to describe the product you are selling: color/measurement/material/purpose.

**Q:** How do I figure out the right target audiences for my items?

**A:** Create customer personas, getting their demographics based on past orders.

**Q:** How to ship items for low cost?

**A:** For products under 2lb, the lowest shipping rate will be from United States Postal Service. For heavier products, go with FedEx or UPS.

**Q:** How can I make my business sustainable and continue to grow?

**A:** Attend conferences and seminars to get updates and new ideas for your business.

For example here's my course - Million Dollar Golden Formula

http://ellenpro.com/course/million-dollar-golden-formula/

**Q:** How can I connect with successful e-commerce operators?

**A:** Attend networking events and conferences.

**Q:** How would you help a diet product rise above the noise and sound trustworthy?

**A:** Get testimonial videos

**Q:** Tips for starting small

**A:** Control your budget. Don't buy hundreds of units per SKU before you test the product.

## Challenges and Motivation

**Q:** What is the most important fundamental that got you to where you are today!

**A:** A growth mindset

**Q:** How did you motivate yourself to become a successful business owner!

**A:** Reading

**Q:** What's the best way to learn entrepreneurial mindset?

**A:** Reading. Study Tony Robbins, Tai Lopez, Jack Canfield, Seth Godin, and etc.

**Q:** How do you stay focused and become consistent

**A:** Set daily goals

**Q:** What was your greatest challenge?

**A:** Employee management, it's still a tough lesson.

**Q:** How can I have a successful business and still spend time with my family?

**A:** Delegate more.

**Q:** How can I be successful like you?

**A:** Hire Ellen as a mentor.

# CHAPTER 11

# Where do you go from here?
# The Sky's the Limit

## Finding the Time and Energy

Now that you have read through this book you know what you can do? So what's stopping you?

Here's what people tell me:

I can't seem to squeeze in some extra hours to do these tasks.

And there are so many different things in my head that need to be executed.

I don't know where to start first. I get frustrated so I keep procrastinating.

After a few months, I still haven't started anything yet!

You are not alone. That was exactly how I felt when I first started Ellenpro.

I was running two businesses already- an e-commerce business and a manufacturing business that required me to work at night to communicate with Asia and Europe. The e-commerce business grew rapidly and I had to quit my martial arts class.

Even though I had hired additional help, I now had no time to keep my body in shape.

Now I was starting a third business in a completely new realm. Most people probably wouldn't even consider it. But I'm just too hungry for greater success, and I was strongly motivated to build a platform to help people learn about success.

Was I stressed? Being an entrepreneur, I'm used to the idea that things might go wrong sometimes. But I know that no matter if it's people, computers, money, products, or my own mistakes. Everything has a solution, so I don't let it bother me as much. The only thing that really stressed me out was that I was making no progress on things I wanted to achieve, and I couldn't find a solution for that.

I needed more time to exercise, learn, read, and work on Ellenpro. I tried to do it at night. But my body and brain didn't function so well because my days were overwhelmed with the two businesses I was already running. So I couldn't produce good outcomes.

Time management was my biggest issue, and I knew that. But I was still struggling until I read this book *The Miracle Morning: The Not-So-Obvious Secret Guaranteed to Transform Your Life (Before 8AM)* by Hal Elrod

I took action immediately.

Here's what I did:

I started waking up ONE HOUR earlier than my usual time every day, including weekends.

You can do this too and with the following four steps you can move yourself to another level.

## Plan Ahead and Auto-Suggest The Night Before (15 minutes)

Before I go to sleep each night, I jot down what I want to achieve in the following day in my Evernote. And then I gave myself an auto-suggestion - *I'm going to have a good night sleep with enough rest.* By doing this, your brain will be programmed and you will not feel like you do not have enough sleep when you wake up.

## Morning Meditation (4 Minutes)

In the morning when I wake up, I sit on my bed and take a few minutes to meditate.

First, I think about my goals and visualize them. Then I give myself another auto-suggestion that I will accomplish certain steps toward those goals today.

Secondly, I feel grateful for everything and everyone around me

## Hydration

Then I walk to downstairs and drink one full glass of water.

Scientists have shown a research that dehydration makes people feeling tired. So one full glass of water will make you awake.

## Exercise And Read - No this does not mean read emails

Do not check your emails or social media at all. You need to own this one hour of yours completely. You live by other people's schedule if you reply e-mails or social networks messages.

After breakfast (the breakfast time was included in my original wake up time, so I didn't count it in the additional hour I have), I do the following:

First - Exercise. For me, it's Tabata workout (4 minutes); Second - Read and cycle on my mini cycle at the same time (15 minutes). I do exercising and reading together a two-fer.

Now I'm all sweated and energized by the workout and my dopamine* level is high. Now I can start doing some blogging effectively. For you, it could be anything you want to achieve that you couldn't find time to do before (the power is in this 41 minutes – this is your time to move forward).

*\* "Dopamine is a neurotransmitter that helps control the brain's reward and pleasure centers. Dopamine also helps regulates movement and emotional responses, and it enables us not only to see rewards, but to take action to move toward them. "Psychology Today*

Do you see how much you can accomplish in an hour? What's the #1 thing you want to achieve but you couldn't find the time to do so? Here's your hour to do it in. No excuses.

Even if you're not a morning person, it's okay.

Even though the book says it's before 8am, you can wake up anytime - just one hour earlier than your usual time will help you a lot.

Because of the morning exercise, my day goes so smooth and I accomplish everything I planned with a good mood.

At the early stage of my business, as I've told you, I did a lot of things wrong.

I wasted tons of money on the wrong products, wrong advertisement, wrong business operations. I spent many years to figure out everything, and found the most effective solutions over time.

I kept at it because I was sure of my goal.

Now that you've read what I've been through and what it takes, here's the question you have to ask yourself - Do you really want to make tons of money online, and become a millionaire?

If you're interested in selling online or you want to boost up your sales, I can help you. I've experienced everything you're going to experience, and I bet I already know the solution to your biggest struggles. Based on my success and experience over the past 6 years, I have built a step-by step system to guide you to the success you desire!

You might wonder, why would I share my biggest secrets and teach you?

I had a woman ask me this and it made me think. She said that she knows a lot of online selling instructors, they are making money by teaching, simply because their own online store doesn't make much money. I finally understood how I am different to all the other online instructors who teach selling online.

Because today, right now at this moment. I'm still running my online store. And my online store business is growing every year.

Many people who are successful in e-commerce but are not willing to share any of their secrets because they're afraid they're teaching their competitors. So, why am I teaching you my secrets? Because my business is growing steadily and I've already found an automatic system to keep growing. I delegate most of the tasks to my employees, and now I have extra time to do this thing that I love.

I saw that there were many people who trying to succeed by selling online but they just couldn't do it, so they felt discouraged.

I knew that I had the answers for them but didn't know how I could communicate them. One day, I saw this Facebook ad about how to teach online – yes a Facebook ad. That's how I found my way to teaching my expertise, to help and empower people to achieve financial and time freedom by selling online.

Once my students followed the course material they started getting great results. Their lives changed and I got to be a part of it. I could feel their excitement and momentum. I realized that it means even more to me than my own success. I'm excited with myself for making a million dollars, but I feel so much more when my students start making 6 figures or more.

So this is my mission. I want to use my knowledge and success to help and empower more people like you, to achieve financial and time freedom. That's why I built this training course called Million Dollar Golden Formula.
http://ellenpro.com/course/million-dollar-golden-formula/

The course is everything you need to start making a profitable online store today.

It's ALL the secret strategies I used to build my own million dollar online store from $600.

If you've read all the way through this book you now know the basics and I've already shown you that it's easy to understand.

What's next for you?

Maximize, Master, Mentor

Join the Community of Successful Entrepreneurs

If you want to go further, I am here to teach you and coach you.

The sky's the limit!

# Glossary

**Algorithm**

In e-commerce this means how each marketplace populates the product search result.

**Amazon**

The biggest and the fastest growing online marketplace.

**Amazon Prime**

As an online shopper if you purchase Amazon Prime annual membership, you get to enjoy 2-day free shipping.

**Brand**

A category of products that are made or carried by a particular company.

**E-Bay**

One of the biggest online marketplaces

**Fulfillment**

Shipping physical products to consumers.

**FBA – Fulfillment by Amazon**

As a seller Amazon helps you to ship physical products to your buyers.

## Key Words

The text you input in the search box when you look for a product on a marketplace.

## Marketplace

A website that allows you to buy and sell products.

## Platform

An operating system on computers.

## Private Label

You buy existing products from manufactures directly, and re-sell them as your own brand.

## Product Line

A category of products

## SEM

Search engine marketing - a form of internet marketing that increases the visibility in the search engine result such as Google.com

## SEO

Search engine optimization - a form of internet marketing by using repeated keywords that increases the visibility in the search engine result such as Google.com

## Shopify

An online platform that allows you to build an e-commerce webstore.

## SKUs

Stock keeping units, products.

## Squeeze Box

Squeeze box is a pop-out window from your web store that collects people's email

## Templates

A pre-formatted webstore setup that you can plug and use.

# Connect With Ellen Lin

Website:        Ellenpro.com

LinkedIn:       linkedin.com/in/ellenlin

Facebook:       facebook.com/ellenpro.entrepreneur

Instagram:      instagram.com/ellenpro_entrepreneur

Twitter:        twitter.com/lin_ellenpro

YouTube:        goo.gl/5oqBjw

# Enter to win:

"30 Minute Strategy Call with Ellen"

Congratulations on taking your time to finish this book. As a thank you, here's a bonus – a 30 Minute Strategy Call. You get a chance to talk to me in person, ask me to solve your challenges and I will personally design your action plans (step-by-step) towards your goal.

Visit ellenpro.com/gift/ now for details to win the 30 Minute Strategy Call with Ellen.

Made in the USA
Monee, IL
06 March 2021